Sergei Tchoban

Architecture Drawings

Sergei Tchoban
Architecture Drawings

Edited by
Luca Molinari

Introductions by
Santiago Calatrava
Massimiliano Fuksas

SKIRA

Editor
Luca Molinari

Art Director
Marcello Francone

Design
Luigi Fiore

Editing
Emily Ligniti

Layout
Paola Ranzini

Translations
Sergio Knipe for *Scriptum*, Rome

First published in Italy in 2015 by
Skira Editore S.p.A.
Palazzo Casati Stampa
via Torino 61
20123 Milano
Italy
www.skira.net

Printed and bound in Italy. First edition

ISBN: 978-88-572-2542-5

Distributed in USA, Canada, Central & South America by Rizzoli International Publications, Inc., 300 Park Avenue South, New York, NY 10010, USA.
Distributed elsewhere in the world by Thames and Hudson Ltd., 181A High Holborn, London WC1V 7QX, United Kingdom.

Contents

The Inner Sight

When I first had the opportunity to admire the drawings so beautifully illustrated in this volume published by Skira, I was gripped by emotion.

As I leafed through the text, I realized that my feelings were not simply due to the remarkable quality of the drawings, in which a dense yet graceful hand brings monuments and landscapes of unquestionable beauty to the reader's attention. The emotion I was experiencing had deeper roots, connected to the land the authors have chosen as their field of research and testing ground. I am speaking of Italy and its remarkable art cities.

What emerges from these drawings by Sergei Tchoban is a desire to reclaim the original matrix of each work through the rendering of some of the most famous and interesting monuments in Italy, in such a way as to digest its components and get to the very roots of contemporary art.

To achieve this goal, Sergei Tchoban would appear to have drawn upon that "inner sight" described by Wassily Kandinsky, a sight which "penetrates the hard shell, the external form, into the interior of things and lets us perceive the inner pulsation of things with all our senses."

The collection of drawings featured here exudes the same feeling which inspired the great artists of the past to visit Italy, as illustrated by Stendhal in *Rome, Naples et Florence*, by Goethe in *Italienische Reise* or, indeed, by Joseph Brodsky when he speaks of the city of Venice in his poem *Lagoon*: "Mouldings and carvings, palaces and flights / of stairs. Look up: the lion smiles from heights / of a tower wrapped as in a coat / of wind". This is the same city that Charles Dickens, after visiting St Mark's Square and its church, described to his friend John Forster as sumptuous and amazing, beyond all human imagination.

But celebrated modern writers are not alone in attesting to the charm of Italian architecture.

During the time he spent in Italy working on the set designs for the Russian ballet *Parade* – written by Cocteau and directed by Diaghilev – Picasso was strongly influenced by his visits to ancient monuments in Rome, Florence, Naples and Pompeii. From that moment, down to the mid-1920s, Picasso's encounter with ancient art shaped his oeuvre, as is shown by many works from this so-called "classical" period of his career, including the splendid *Flute de Pan*. Just like the Russian architect who is the author of the works illustrated in the present volume, during his short sojourn in Italy – where he met his great love, Olga Khokhlova – Picasso could not resist the impulse to capture the charm of the country's monuments through sketches and drawings.

I, myself, during my frequent trips to the capital of Italy, have behaved much like the Roman prince from Gogol's novel, who "each day would set out to discover new marvels and . . . stop when in a small piazza he chanced upon a picturesque fountain . . . or when a dark, dirty street ended with the playful architecture of Bernini, with a flying obelisk, with a church and the wall of a monastery which burst in the sun's brilliance on the dark azure sky, with cypresses black as coal. And the more he travelled the streets, the more palaces and architectural works by Bramante, Borromini, Sangallo, Della Porta, Vignola and Buonarroti emerged. Finally, he understood that only here, in Italy, does the presence of architecture become tangible."

No doubt, Italy is one of the most exemplary countries from the point of view of architecture, since it boasts a genuine historical repertoire for all the various ages in which architecture has played a fundamental role. This extends as far back as the Roman age, which has left grand works such as aqueducts, thermal baths, mausoleums and many other urban structures that are still to be found in Italian cities. Ultimately, Italy may be described as a country which has made its practice of architecture an exemplary one and which represents one of the world's leading schools for urban architecture.

On every visit I make to Italy, I will peer into the dense fabric of its art cities to discover a marble pediment set in a wall, a Doric column supporting a medieval architrave or a highly decorated baroque window. Pondering this prodigious mingling of styles, like the author of the sketches illustrated in this volume, I seek to capture the most concealed images and messages by drawing the founding elements of contemporaneity from the complex juxtaposition of different architectural languages. These repeated experiences, which I process through impromptu sketches and drawings, expand my own cultural background, while at the same time teach me to be humble in my own artistic pursuits.

Still, it is worth stressing that this constant drawing upon the roots of civilization on the part of modern and contemporary artists also entails a degree of profound reciprocity. If we take Russian artists, it is easy to see just how influential the music of Tchaikovsky, Stravinsky, Shostakovich and Prokofiev has been for twentieth-century European art. Likewise, the revolutionary ideas of Kandinsky and the movement he championed, Der blaue Reiter, paved the way for Bauhaus, the modern architecture movement which re-established a connection between art and real life. Or let us think here of how Vladimir Tatlin's Russian constructivism and Kazimir Malevich's early, visionary drawings inspired the young Antonio Sant'Elia, the author of the "Manifesto of Futurist Architecture".

One last point concerns the message that comes from the exhibition of these drawings. As Jean Dominique Ingres, Director of the French Academy in Italy, liked to say: "Le dessin c'est la probité dans l'art". In a particularly delicate political moment such as the present one – in which the peoples of the West seem to have no memory of the damage and atrocities of past wars, and governments are fuelling a dangerous escalation by issuing reciprocal sanctions – the commitment displayed by Sergei Tchoban through the depiction of the artworks from a foreign country delivers a powerful message of integrity and peace. Such peace finds in the universal quality of art its lifeblood, and in the cultural exchange between different peoples its sole chance for survival.

Santiago Calatrava

**"When once we see keenly enough,
there is very little difficulty in drawing what we see"***

I have had my hands upon drawings by Alessandro Galli Bibiena (Parma 1686 – Mannheim 1748). It was one of the most important feelings that I have ever experienced. The expressive power of a drawing is not comparable to the amount of pictures that, without any passions or upheaval, are shot, or rather generated as an unexpected gust of wind. Drawing as memory. We recognize and sometimes we learn to know the places that have been crossed throughout history, thanks to different interpretations over time. The first trip to Rome made by Filippo Brunelleschi in 1402 with his friend Donatello was to observe, study and copy what remained of Antiquity, from which to draw inspiration, which leads to the discovery of new expressive potentiality. Palladio, who stayed in the same city between 1541 and 1544, gathered from the reconstructions of Roman Baths the basic elements for the construction of his own buildings. One might add that the Italian eighteenth century provided the instrument of drawing with the right continuity by the genius and the quick notes of Borromini, most of them preserved at the Albertina in Vienna. Collecting drawings and notes is not only the best way to create a synthesis between vision and passion. It is also the selective choice of what a day, a moment, a moment in the life of a creator gives generously to others. It makes a world of hurried people participant to the infinite passion that touch produces and the choice of what their vision of reality conveys. Sergei Tchoban was born in Leningrad (now St Petersburg). After graduating in Architecture in that city, he moved to Hamburg and Berlin. In 2006, he founded the studio SPEECH in Moscow, along with Sergey Kuznetsov. In 2009, he designed the Tchoban Foundation – Museum for Architectural Drawing, which was opened in Berlin in 2013. An important collection of drawings from the seventeenth to the twenty-first century testify his great love and dedication and commitment to supporting young talents.

The drawings in this book form the vocabulary that one needs to compose, where the present becomes the container of the past and the future. Drawing is a way to tell a project. Travel notes where with skill, confidence and irony also emerge in the city's soul as *White Nights of St Petersburg* (in pastel, 2007). Or the echoes of classical Antiquity are well represented in the drawing of the *Pantheon* (watercolour and ink, 2006). So the images of a fantastical world, an expression of a thought that each of us can share, as in the interesting series of "New study on the relationship between water and architecture" (ink and watercolour, 1997). The space evoked is always represented realistically. The philosopher Zeno, in the fifth century BC, in one of his paradoxes tells us of the arrow which, once shot, analysed conceptually in its trajectory space, time, it also stops and remains suspended in space. One could say that between one point and the other there is a mental chasm that no bridge can join. In these areas, there are other worlds. The infinite cannot be contained. Thought emigrates, travels, it is eternal. Ideas are circular and are transmitted by contact.

Massimiliano Fuksas

* John Ruskin

Luca Molinari

A Dialogue with Sergei Tchoban

LM: *As a designer, you have invested a significant amount of time making hundreds of drawings within the last two decades. What does drawing mean to you? When did you begin to consider drawing as a relevant part of your background and education?*
ST: I began drawing on a regular basis, as early as my schooldays, and of course, continued during my studies at the academy. For me, architectural drawing is a whole and discrete genre by which I am able to express my thoughts on space, detail, surface – basically, on everything that constitutes architecture.

LM: *Analysing your drawings, I cannot find a direct relationship with your work, but I am sure that your research on drawings nurtures your research as a designer. Could you explain how drawing fosters and influences your design process?*
ST: With my drawings, I examine urban layers, the historical build-up of places, including their accumulation, debris, traces, losses . . . The most important aspect for me, while doing this, is to identify the role of contemporary architecture with its very specific means of expression, when it builds up these layers. How does the new correspond with the old? What makes old architecture captivate us? That's what I'm after when I'm drawing.

LM: *Studying your drawings, a relationship and a form of continuity with the generations of Russian artists and architects who considered Italy and Europe as a centre for their research and inspiration is evident. Do you feel this continuity? And which kind of relationship do you perceive with contemporary experiences?*
ST: I suppose, not only Russian but all architects studied Italy – and all of Europe – in order to learn from the past and then to identify their own style, their specific architectural idiom. To create something new means at first to find out who you are, and then to get an idea of what can be considered valuable. For me, personally, it means relating to the richness of texture, its content and density, both in the historical dimension and the contemporary one. This dialogue is my focus in drawing.

LM: *You've devoting a significant part of your life to promoting architectural drawings by collecting them, saving important archives and creating a foundation of architectural drawing. Why do you think it is so important to save and promote the art of architectural drawing today? And what do you think should be the role of drawing in contemporary architecture and culture?*
ST: Architectural drawing will always be the official language of an architect, whereas computers help us – to a continuously growing extent – to carry out a project. But even today, people are still fascinated by looking at hand-drawn images. We can see this by the rising numbers of museum visitors at our exhibitions and their comments.

LM: *I feel that for you drawing is a personal, joyful obsession. Could you describe your approach over one day devoted to drawing? How and why do you choose the point of view and the positioning of your drawings?*
ST: I usually choose what I find interesting, sometimes more subconsciously than purposefully.

And that subliminal way of acting, tracking my thoughts on paper, is what I enjoy the most.

LM: *In your work and approach, drawing is much more than an aesthetic, but it represents a way of looking and analysing the city and its character. Could you describe the relationship between drawings and your vision of the urban environment?*
ST: Analysing the layers of the cityscape is the most important aspect. Why does a certain architecture tend to age better, and others not? What are the influences of different ages on each other in a single spot? How can they be regulated or manipulated?

LM: *Which role should drawing play in the architectural education and in the architect's training today?*
ST: I cannot repeat it often enough: for young architects, drawing is a tremendously important way to find out what excites them about architecture, and therefore it is an essential subject in their education.

LM: *An interesting section of your drawings is devoted to imaginary cities, where water often seems to play a quintessential role, creating illusions of the double and mirroring ancient cities. Could you consider those "follies" as a free field of research? Which meanings and values do you attach to this category of drawings?*
ST: Architectural fantasies are actually the results of my field studies. They convey my ideas of what the urban fabric, structures, places and objects could consist of today or in the future: spaces and ages, structures and decay, overlappings and gaps, depths and limits, and so forth.

Windowsill, 2009
Sepia ink, watercolour, pencil on paper, 31 × 40 cm

Sketchbook, Diaries and Observational

White Nights 3, 2007
Charcoal on paper, 30 × 40 cm

The Pantheon, Rome, 2009
Charcoal on paper, 25 × 35 cm

The Pantheon, Rome, 2006
Watercolour, Indian ink on paper, 53 × 72 cm

Courtyard in Montecatini Terme, 2005
Pencil, pastel, watercolour on paper, 32 × 41 cm

Seu de Palma, Cathedral of Palma de Mallorca, 2007
Indian ink, watercolour on paper, 67 × 41 cm

Architectural study, 1994
Pencil on paper, 41 × 45 cm

Cathedral of Amalfi, 2006
Pastel, pencil on paper, 40 × 32 cm

Granada, 2007
Pastel, pencil on paper, 57 × 39 cm

Backyard in Sorrento, 2006
Pastel on paper, 60 × 40 cm

VLTOR
IA

St Petersburg courtyard
near the Vladimir belfry, 2008
Watercolour, pencil on paper, 30 × 40 cm

The Pantheon, Rome, 2008
Indian ink, watercolour on paper, 51 × 67 cm

Sant'Andrea della Valle, Rome, 2008
Sepia ink, watercolour on paper, 40 × 29 cm

Venice, 2008
Charcoal on grey paper, 40 × 60 cm

Catalonia, 2008
Charcoal on paper, 25 × 34 cm

Brooklyn Bridge, New York City, 2009
Charcoal on paper, 27 × 19 cm

Fifth Avenue and Central Park, New York City, 2009
Pencil on paper, 27 × 20 cm

Sevilla, 2011
Bistre ink on paper, 41 × 31 cm

Siena, 2011
Indian ink, watercolour on paper, 35.6 × 53.6 cm

Amiens Cathedral, France, 2009
Indian ink, watercolour on paper, 64 × 50 cm

St Gatien, Tours, 2009
Sepia ink, watercolour on paper, 60 × 40 cm

Piazza dei Signori, Verona, 2010
Sepia ink, watercolour on paper, 39 × 55 cm

City in the snow, 2010
Charcoal, pastel on paper, 39 × 32 cm

City in the snow, 2010
Charcoal, pastel on paper, 39 × 32 cm

City in the snow, 2010
Charcoal, pastel on paper, 39 × 32 cm

City in the snow, 2010
Charcoal, pastel on paper, 39 × 32 cm

Cathedral in Brasilia, 2012
Grey ink on paper, 31 × 40.8 cm

Museum by Oscar Niemeyer, Niterói, 2012
Grey ink on paper, 31 × 40.6 cm

San Galgano, 2011
Sepia ink, watercolour on paper, 55 × 38 cm

Cordoba, Spain, 2011
Sepia ink on paper, 55.8 × 37.5 cm

City of gods, Teotihuacán, Mexico, 2012
Pastel on paper, 56 × 62 cm

San Satiro, Milan, 2012
Sepia ink on paper, 60.2 × 40.1 cm

Brügge, 2013
Sepia watercolour on paper, 59 × 35 cm

Singapore, 2013
Pastel, charcoal on paper, 33 × 41 cm

New York Central Station, 2011
Black and white pastel on grey paper, 30.5 × 23 cm

Mantua, 2014
Sepia ink, watercolour on paper, 59.5 × 39.3 cm

Lucca, 2014
Sepia ink, watercolour on paper, 39.5 × 59.5 cm

Water and the City

Two fluids, two realities, 2001
Indian ink, watercolour on paper, 60 × 43 cm

Underwater scenario on the pages of a trashy novel, 2002
Felt-tip pen, pencil on paper, 17 × 10 cm

Diary sketches, 2002
Indian ink, coloured pencil on paper, 17 × 20 cm

Page from the diary I, 2002
Pencil, felt-tip pen, crayon, ink on paper,
27 × 38 cm

Page from the diary II, 2002
Pencil, felt-tip pen, crayon, ink on paper,
39 × 27 cm

Diary pages, 2002
Pencil, felt-tip pen, coloured pencil,
ink on paper, 27 × 38 cm

Page from the diary III, 2002
Pencil, felt-tip pen, crayon, ink on paper,
38 × 27 cm

Lock of the Moskva-Volga Canal I, 2001
Indian ink, watercolour on paper, 35 × 56 cm

Lock of the Moskva-Volga Canal II, 2001
Indian ink, watercolour on paper, 35 × 56 cm

Lock of the Moskva-Volga Canal III, 2001
Indian ink, watercolour on paper, 55 × 37 cm

Urban maritime vision with Palladian and modern motifs, 1992
Charcoal on paper, 65 × 47 cm

Water worlds 2, 1995
Indian ink on paper, 36 × 32 cm

Water worlds 3, 1995
Indian ink, watercolour on paper, 32 × 37 cm

Water worlds 4, 1995
Indian ink, watercolour on paper, 37 × 32 cm

Underwater settlement, 2002
Pencil, felt-tip pen, coloured pencil,
Indian ink on paper, 40 × 14 cm

St Martin Cathedral in Lucca, 2005
Pencil, pastel on paper, 32 × 41 cm

Function hall for 200 persons, 2005
Pastel on paper, 50 × 65 cm

Клуб на 300 мест
С. Чобан 2005

Reminiscence of Santa Maria della Salute in Venice, 1993
Pastel chalk on paper, 56 × 26 cm

Baroque City in water, 2004
Watercolour, Indian ink on paper, 41 × 30 cm

St Petersburg dream II, 2005
Charcoal, watercolour on paper, 30 × 40 cm

White Nights of St Petersburg, 2005
Charcoal, watercolour on paper, 44 × 61 cm

St Petersburg dream I: Five corners, 2005
Charcoal, watercolour on paper, 40 × 28 cm

St Petersburg fantasy, 2007
Watercolour, charcoal on paper, 43 × 65 cm

Lock of the Moskva-Volga Canal IV, 2001
Indian ink, watercolour on paper, 54 × 34 cm

Baroque city in the water, 2004
Indian ink, watercolour on paper, 30 × 41 cm

White Nights of St Petersburg, 2007
Pastel on paper, 54 × 76 cm

Simple forms, 1998
Indian ink, watercolour on paper, 66 × 46 cm

Italian cityscape, 2006
Indian ink, watercolour on paper, 42 × 60 cm

Waterside city, 2008
Ballpoint pen on paper, 30 × 21 cm

Aqua (triptych), 2008

Left part of the triptych *Aqua*, 2008
Pencil on paper, 27 × 19 cm

Central part of the triptych *Aqua*, 2008
Pencil on paper, 27 × 19 cm

Right part of the triptych *Aqua*, 2008
Pencil on paper, 27 × 19 cm

Temple in the water, 2008
Pencil on paper, 19 × 27 cm

Waters, 2009
Sepia ink, watercolour, pencil on paper, 32 × 54 cm

Untitled (polyptych), 2009

Upper left part of an untitled polyptych, 2009
Sepia ink, watercolour, pencil on paper,
31 × 40 cm

Windowsill, upper right part
of an untitled polyptych, 2009
Sepia ink, watercolour, pencil on paper, 31 × 40 cm

St Petersburg, snowy 1, lower left part
of an untitled polyptych, 2009
Watercolour, Indian ink, pencil on paper, 31 × 40 cm

St Petersburg, snowy 2, lower right part
of an untitled polyptych, 2009
Sepia ink, watercolour on paper, 31 × 40 cm

Greek church with dome, 2004
Charcoal on paper, 26 × 31 cm

A fantasy drawing for the exhibition Stalin today, 2011
Pastel on paper, 21 × 29.6 cm

Baroque scene, 2011
Pastel on paper, 65 × 50 cm

Baroque scene, 2011
Pastel on paper, 65 × 50 cm

Baroque scene, 2011
Pastel on paper, 65 × 50 cm

Baroque scene, 2011
Pastel on paper, 65 × 50 cm

Design of a film set, Waterfall No. 3, 2011
Watercolour, ink on paper, 37 × 56 cm

Design of a film set, Waterfall No. 1, 2011
Watercolour, ink on paper, 37 × 55 cm

Landmark Design for the Zhuhai Hengqin Chimelong Ocean Resort in China, 2012
Watercolour, ink on paper, 65 × 50 cm

Design of a film set, Waterfall No. 2, 2011
Watercolour, ink on paper, 55 × 37 cm

Architectural Fantasy I, 2012
Watercolour, Indian ink on paper, 60 × 40 cm

Sunken City, 2009
Watercolour, Indian ink on paper, 38 × 55 cm

Architectural Fantasy II, 2012
Watercolour, Indian ink on paper, 40 × 50 cm

Visions, Follies and Fantasies

Moscow, the underground city,
protected from the atom bomb, 2003
Felt-tip pen, pencil on paper, 21 × 30 cm

Architectural fantasy: Lenin's head, 2003
Felt-tip pen, pencil on paper, 21 × 17 cm

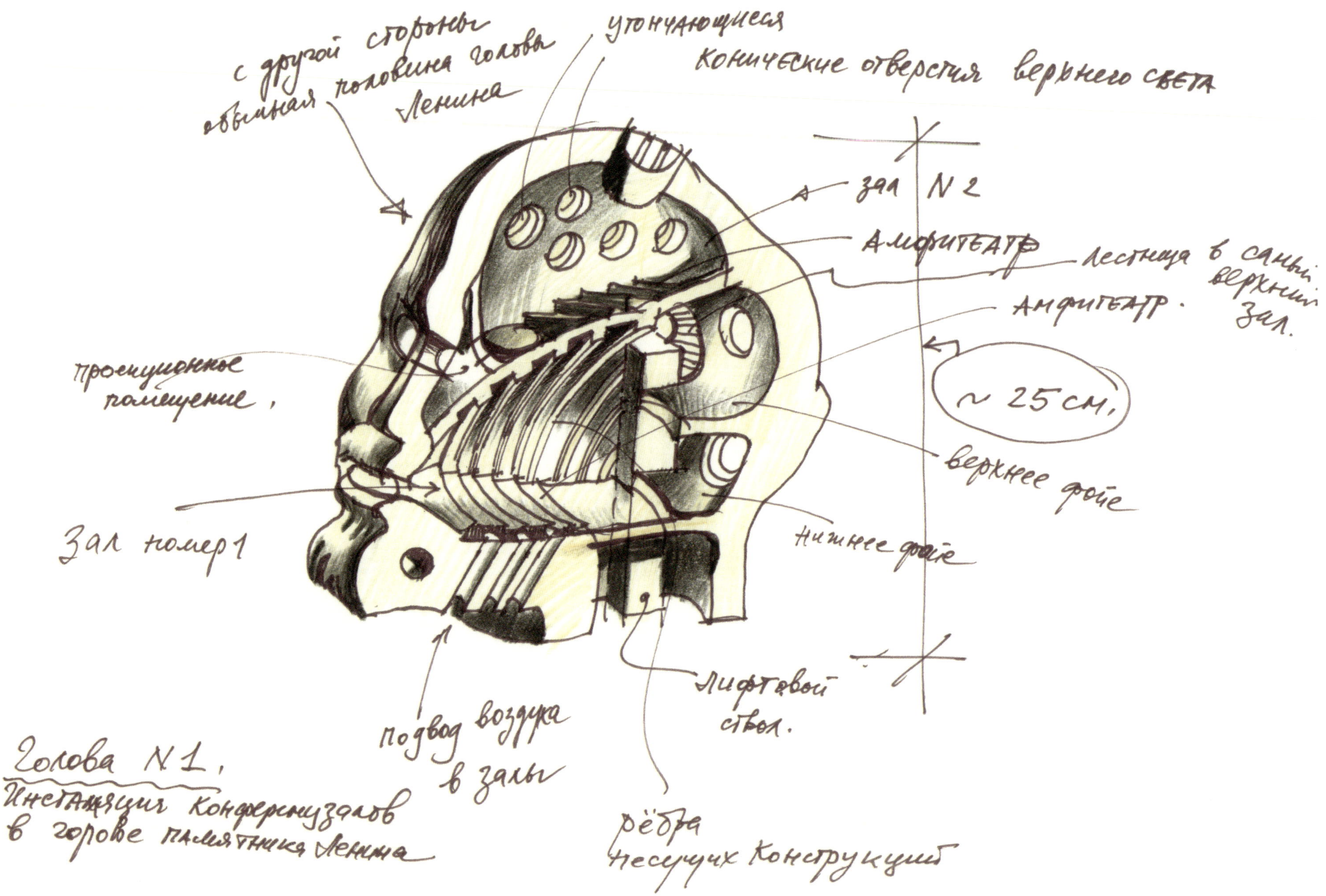

Architectural fantasy: Lenin, 2003
Indian ink, coloured pencil on paper, 21 × 29 cm

Staging for the exhibition
STADTanSICHTEN – Planschrank Moskau:
Ort einer Hauptstadt, 2003
Felt-tip pen, coloured pencil on paper, 21 × 29 cm

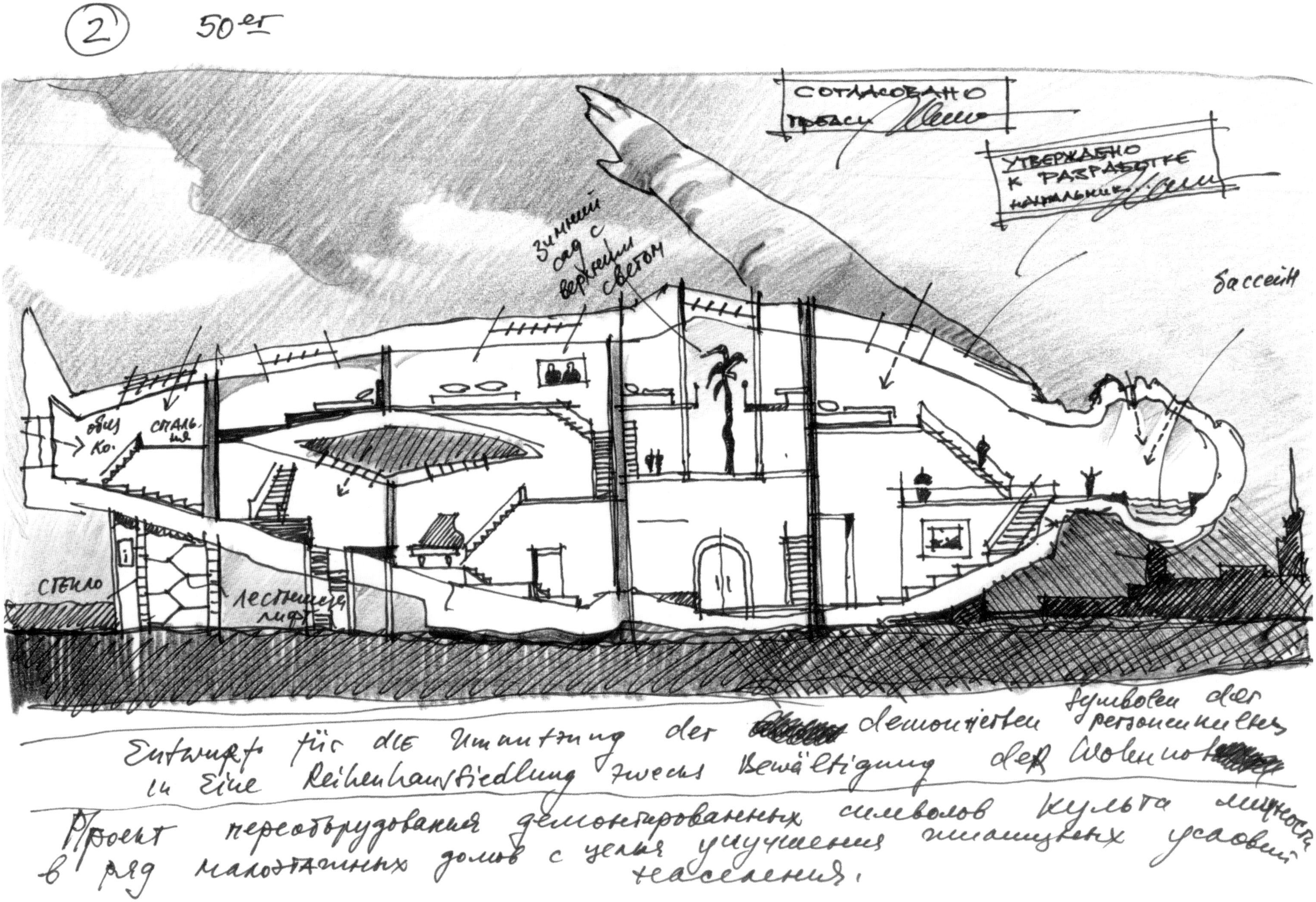

Architectural fantasy: Fallen Statue, 2003
Indian ink, coloured pencil on paper,
21 × 29 cm

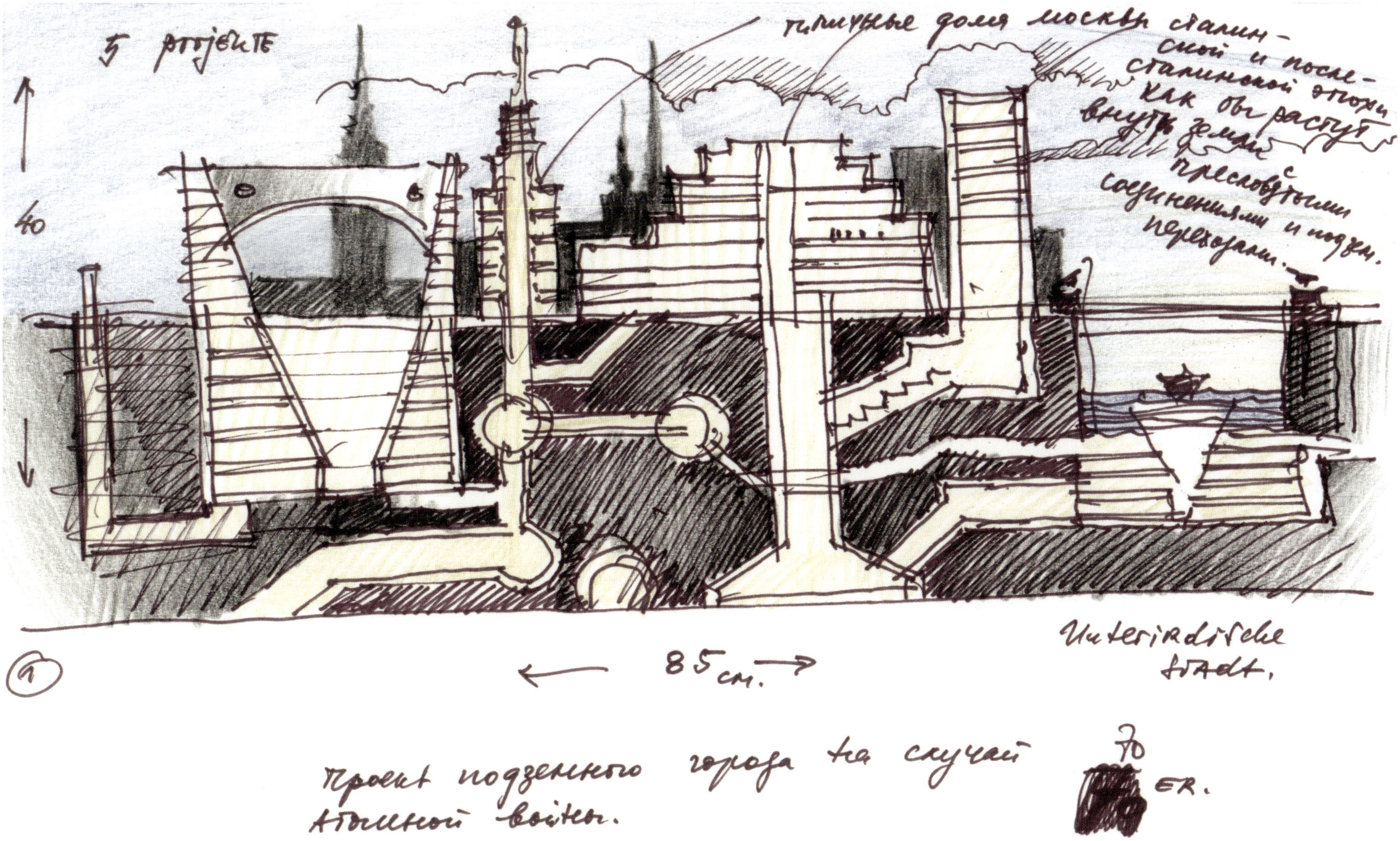

Moscow excavated, 2003
Pencil, felt-tip pen, coloured pencil on paper,
21 × 30 cm

Water worlds 1, 1995
Indian ink, watercolour on paper, 37 × 32 cm

Lenin from above and below, 1994
Indian ink, watercolour on paper, 34 × 34 cm

Space study for the transept of Leipzig central station, 1994
Indian ink, watercolour on paper, 34 × 34 cm

Reality is Truth, Art is Beauty, 2002
Indian ink, watercolour on paper, 56 × 39 cm

Venice, drowning pictures, 2006
Charcoal on paper, 59 × 42 cm

Ponte Vecchio 1, 1998
Indian ink, watercolour on paper, 45 × 65 cm

Old and new street façade in Johannisviertel, Berlin, connected with transparent bridges I, 1999
Indian ink, watercolour on paper, 24 × 100 cm

Old and new street façade in Johannisviertel,
Berlin, connected with transparent bridges III, 1999
Indian ink, watercolour on paper, 24 × 100 cm

Architectural fantasy on the Dubinivskaya Street office complex, Moscow, 2007
Charcoal on paper, 65 × 50 cm

Composite image of the Frauenkirche in Dresden, 1994
Pencil, watercolour on paper, 55 × 44 cm

Rising waters, 1996
Indian ink, watercolour on paper, 48 × 46 cm

Wrong dimensioning: Academy of Arts, Milan, 2008
Pastel, sepia ink, watercolour on grey paper,
25 × 34 cm

Wrong dimensioning: Milan, 2008
Pastel, sepia ink, watercolour on grey paper,
34 × 25 cm

Wrong dimensioning: stairs of the Pinacoteca di Brera, Milan, 2008
Pastel, sepia ink, watercolour, pencil on grey paper, 34 × 25 cm

Backyard studies of the Johannis Quarter, 1999
Indian ink, watercolour on paper, 59 × 58 cm

Vertical composition of bridges and stairs, infinitely growing (polyptych), 2009

Bottom part of the polyptych
Vertical composition of bridges and stairs, infinitely growing, 2009
Pencil, sepia ink on paper, 32 × 40 cm

Lower central part of the polyptych
Vertical composition of bridges and stairs, infinitely growing, 2009
Pencil, sepia ink on paper, 32 × 40 cm

Upper central part of the polyptych
Vertical composition of bridges and stairs, infinitely growing, 2009
Pencil, sepia ink on paper, 32 × 40 cm

Top part of the polyptych *Vertical composition of bridges and stairs, infinitely growing*, 2009
Pencil, sepia ink on paper, 32 × 40 cm

City windows (polyptych), 2009

Top left part of the polyptych *City windows*, 2009
Pastel, pencil on coloured paper, 27 × 19 cm

Top right part the polyptych *City windows*, 2009
Pastel, pencil on coloured paper, 27 × 19 cm

Bottom left part of the polyptych *City windows*, 2009
Pastel, pencil on coloured paper, 27 × 19 cm

Bottom right part of the polyptych *City windows*, 2009
Pastel, pencil on coloured paper, 27 × 19 cm

Fantasy drawing for the project of the Museum for Architectural Drawing or: Evolution of form 3, 2010
Charcoal on paper, 53 × 34 cm

Fantasy drawing for the project of the Museum for Architectural Drawing or: Evolution of form 1, 2010
Charcoal on paper, 40 × 60 cm

Fantasy drawing for the project of the Museum for Architectural Drawing or: Evolution of form 2, 2010
Charcoal on paper, 60 × 40 cm

Museum for Architectural Drawing, 2010
Charcoal on paper, 41 × 32 cm

Venice, Salute at night, 2010
Charcoal and white chalk on paper, 40.4 × 32.2 cm

Architectural capriccio, Forum Romanum
or Two worlds No. 1, film stage design project,
St Petersburg, 2013
Pen, Indian ink, watercolour, pencil on paper,
50 × 70 cm

Architectural capriccio, Piazza Venezia in Rome or Two worlds No. 2, film stage design project, St Petersburg, 2013
Pen, Indian ink, drybrush, watercolour, pencil on paper, 50 × 70 cm

Two worlds No. 3, film stage design project, St Petersburg, 2013
Pencil, watercolour on paper, 57 × 72 cm

Remodelling project of the German pavilion in Venice (polyptych), 2013

Top left part of the polyptych *Remodelling project of the German pavilion in Venice*, 2013
Pencil, Indian ink, watercolour, coloured pencil on paper, 80 × 59 cm

Top right part of the polyptych *Remodelling project of the German pavilion in Venice*, 2013
Pencil, Indian ink, watercolour, coloured pencil on paper, 80 × 59 cm

Bottom left part of the polyptych *Remodelling project of the German pavilion in Venice*, 2013
Pencil, Indian ink, watercolour, coloured pencil on paper, 80 × 59 cm

Bottom right part of the polyptych *Remodelling project of the German pavilion in Venice*, 2013
Pencil, Indian ink, watercolour, coloured pencil on paper, 80 × 59 cm

Two Worlds / Film Stage Project Design,
St Petersburg, 2014
Indian ink, watercolour on paper,
17.5 × 26 cm

Two Worlds / Film Stage Project Design,
St Petersburg, 2014
Indian ink, watercolour on paper,
18 × 26 cm

Film Stage Design: Under Electric Clouds, 2014
Charcoal on paper, 40 × 30 cm

Film Stage Design: Under Electric Clouds, 2014
Charcoal on paper, 56 × 42 cm

Film Stage Design: Under Electric Clouds, 2014
Charcoal on paper, 40 × 30 cm

Film Stage Design: Under Electric Clouds, 2014
Charcoal on paper, 56 × 42 cm

The urban layers 2, 2014
Watercolour, white gouache on paper,
59.8 × 39.8 cm

The urban layers 4, 2014
Watercolour, white gouache on paper,
60 × 40 cm

The urban layers 1, 2014
Watercolour, white gouache on paper,
60 × 40.2 cm

Chicago, 2010
Black coloured pencil on paper,
41.8 × 29.5 cm

The urban layers 3, 2014
Watercolour, white gouache on paper,
59.9 × 39.8 cm

Biography

Sergei Tchoban was born in 1962 in St Petersburg, Russia. Between 1980 and 1986 he studied at the Ilya Repin Institute, Russian Academy of Arts, St Petersburg. From 1986 to 1990 he was involved in practical work as a graduate architect in Russia.
In 1992, he began working with Nietz - Prasch - Sigl, Hamburg, and in 1995 as a partner of Nietz - Prasch - Sigl und Partner Architekten BDA, Hamburg, Berlin, Dresden, heading the Berlin branch. In 2003, they relaunched as nps tchoban voss Architekten BDA, while in 2006 he founded the architectural studio SPEECH in Moscow. In 2009, he established the Tchoban Foundation – Museum for Architectural Drawing in Berlin and in 2010 he opened the studio ST Design.

Completed Projects

2014
Hotel am Nordkopf, new hotel building, Wolfsburg
LP12 Mall of Berlin, new retail complex with apartments, hotel and additional uses in collaboration with Pechtold Architekten, Berlin
Belles Etage Residence, Jägerstraße, Berlin
Techowpromenade 15, forty-six new flats for senior residents, Berlin
Neue Schönhauser 15, remodelling of a listed historic townhouse, Berlin
Speicherstadt Potsdam, new residential complex, Potsdam

2013
Bismarck-Karrée, new commercial and health centre, Berlin
Museum for Architectural Drawing, Tchoban Foundation, new exhibition building, Berlin
Coca Cola Germany, new corporate headquarters, Berlin
Englische Straße 5, new administration building for the Bundesamt für Bauwesen und Raumordnung, Berlin
Zima and Osen Business Centres, new office buildings, at the Seasons Ensemble, St Petersburg
Spira, kitchen series for rational Einbauküchen, Melle
Water Sports Palace, new aquatic stadium for the World University Games 2013, Kazan

2012
12 Architects Design Furniture, series of office furniture for the executive suite, Nayada
Russian pavilion at the XIII Venice Architecture Biennale, Venice
Meininger Hotel Gateway Gardens, new hotel building, Frankfurt
Apartment Koenigsallee, remodelling of a private apartment, Berlin
Penthouse, structural remodelling and complete furnishing of a triplex apartment, St Petersburg

2011
Bank St Petersburg, urban master plan and new administrative headquarters, in collaboration with Evgeny Gerasimov EGP St Petersburg, St Petersburg
Ernst-Reuter-Haus, extension and modernization of an administration complex (listed monument), Berlin
Moa-Bogen, new shopping centre with hotel and car park, Berlin
Ozerkovskaya embankment, new business complex, Moscow
VTB, office interior in the western tower of the Federation Complex, Moscow
Business multifunctional complex Aquamarine on Ozerkovskaya embankment new business complex, Moscow

2010
nhow Berlin, new music and lifestyle hotel, Berlin
Hamburger Hof, remodelling of a historical crafts complex (listed monument), Berlin
Meininger Hotel, new hotel building, Frankfurt
Intercity Hotel at Willi Brandt Airport BER, new hotel building, Berlin
Invalidenstraße 91, new office building for the BVÖD Federal Association for Public Services, Berlin
Tauentzienstraße 5, new retail and office building, Berlin
Villa in Solnechnoye, new private residence, Kurortnyy District, Russia
Villa in Vasilyevo, new private residence, Priozersky District, Russia
Villa Gorki, reconstruction and extension of private residence, Moscow
Office Building at Leninsky prospekt, Moscow
Granatny 6, new residential complex, Moscow
Grünwald Club Skolkovskoye Shosse, new residential complex, Moscow
Five Seas, A-class business centre, Rostov

2009
Adina Hotel Invalidenstraße, new hotel building, Berlin
Stuttgarter Platz 1, new commercial and medical centre, Berlin
Europe Embankment, master plan for a new city quarter, St Petersburg
E-Plus, new corporate headquarters, Düsseldorf
Esplanade by Duravit, series of sanitary accessories, Duravit AG Hornberg
Obukhov Center, remodelling and extension of administration building for the MedSanChast Hospital, St Petersburg
Bettinastraße, design and construction permit for three luxury villas at Dianasee with seventeen flats, in collaboration with Patrick Hellmann Living, Berlin
Khimvolokno Business Centre, remodelling and extension of office building, St Petersburg

2008
Federation Complex, new multifunctional high-rise complex, in collaboration with Prof Peter Schweger Schweger Assoziierte Gesamtplanung Hamburg, Moscow
House by the Sea, new residential complex, in collaboration with Evgeny Gerasimov EGP St Petersburg, St Petersburg
Leto Business Centere, remodelling and extension of manufacturing facility, St Petersburg
Kaiserstraße, new retail and office building, Karlsruhe
Saturn Elberfeld, extension and modernization of existing commercial complex, Wuppertal
Müllerstrasse, new retail and office building, Berlin
Titania-Palast, remodelling of retail areas in historic movie theatre (listed monument), Berlin
Megatorg, new shopping centre, Vladimir

2007
Saturn Europa-Centre, new retail centre, Berlin
Chabad Lubawitsch Centre, remodelling of former transformer station into a synagogue and family centre, Berlin
Adina Apartments Krausenstraße, new apartment hotel building, Berlin
Benois Business Centre, remodelling and extension of manufacturing facility, St Petersburg
Polustrovo, master plan (revision) on former Rossiya manufacturing property, St Petersburg

2006
Langenzipen Business Centre, remodelling and extension of manufacturing facility, St Petersburg
C & A, new corporate headquarters, Düsseldorf
Berolinahaus, remodelling of historic commercial building at Alexanderplatz (listed monument), Berlin
Axel-Springer-Straße 54, remodelling and extension of office building, Berlin

2005
Kurfürstendamm 38/39, new retail and office building, Berlin
Unter den Linden 32-34, remodelling and extension of retail and office building, Berlin
SXF, new roofed walk and landscaping in public access areas to Schönefeld Airport, Berlin

2004
DomAquarée, new city quarter with hotel, residence and office buildings, Berlin
Spreepalais, remodelling and modernization of public areas, Berlin
Tauentzienstraße 18, new retail and office building, Berlin
Wilmersdorfer Strasse 121, new retail and office building, Berlin
Kurfürstendamm 64-65, conversion of retail and office building with movie theatre, Berlin
Berliner Vorstadt, urban master plan for residential quarter, Potsdam
Riem Arcaden, new city quarter and shopping centre, Munich
Polustrovo, urban master plan for former Rossija manufacturing property, St Petersburg

2003
Kronprinzenkarree, new office building with residential lofts, Berlin
Osthafen, urban master plan for disused harbour areas, Berlin

2002
Kontorhaus Novalisstraße, new office building, Berlin
Kurfürstendamm 42 / Mommsenstraße 71, remodelling of retail and office complex, Berlin
nps tchoban voss Berlin, remodelling and extension of office floors, Berlin

2001
Cubix Cinema, new movie theatre at Alexanderplatz, Berlin
Leipziger Platz Carré, urban master plan, Berlin
Karl-Liebknecht-Straße 31, remodelling of façade, Berlin

2000
Kleine Rosenstraße, remodelling of retail and office building, Hamburg
Alfred-Döblin-Haus, remodelling of façade, Berlin

1999
Stern Centre, new shopping centre, residential high-rise building, Potsdam

1998
Arndt Gallery / Aedes Extension, art gallery pavilion, Berlin

1997
Java Turm, conversion of coffee roasting factory to offices and residential lofts, Hamburg
HGH Fragrance Resources, remodelling of entrance and lobby areas, Hamburg

Current Projects

Europe Embankment Project, urban master plan, in collaboration with Evgeny Gerasimov EGP St Petersburg, new hotel building and multi-use complex, St Petersburg (completion 2016)
Dahlemer Weg, three villas and four apartment buildings out of seventeen residential buildings with underground parking, planned for the Cedelia project by Kondor Wessels and Hochtief, Berlin (completion 2015)
Kloster St Georg, modernization of historic manor, new Russian orthodox chapel, Goetschendorf (completion 2014)
Flora Gärten, two new residential loft buildings in residential complex (completion 2014)
Hotels at Berlin Hauptbahnhof, two new hotel buildings, Berlin (completion 2014)
Flottwellpromenade, urban master plan and two out of eleven residences, underground parking, Berlin (completion 2014)
Kronprinzengärten, four out of twelve new semi-detached apartment townhouses, Berlin (completion 2014)
Titanic Hotel Berlin, new hotel building, Berlin (completion 2014)
East Tower of the Federation Complex, Moscow (completion 2015)
Expo-Gate, new trade fair centre, St Petersburg (completion 2014)
Nevskiy City Hall, new administration complex for the city of St Petersburg (completion 2014)
Jewish Traditional School Chabad Lubavitch, new education centre, Berlin (completion 2015)

Awards

2014
German Design Award, in the Communication and Design category by the German Design Council for the building of the Museum for Architectural Drawing, Berlin
The International Architecture Award 2014 by the Chicago Athenaeum Museum for Architecture and Design, for the building of the Museum of Architectural Drawing, Berlin
Special Mention in the Museums category, of the Architizer A+ Awards 2014, for the building of the Museum for Architectural Drawing
Honourable Mention Award at the AIT Award 2014, Frankfurt/Hamburg 2014 for the building of the Museum for Architectural Drawing, Berlin
Jed Morse Juror Rendering Award, Architecture in Perspective 29 of the American Society of Architectural Illustrators ASAI for the Architectural Drawing Two Worlds 1
Building of the Year, second place by readers voting at german-archtitects.com, Stuttgart, for the building of the Museum for Architectural Drawing, Berlin
Joint winner of the AR+D Emerging Architecture Awards 2013, London, for the building of the Museum for Architectural Drawing, Berlin
Shortlisting at the International Hotel & Property Awards 2014, London, for the building of the Music and Lifestyle Hotel nhow Berlin

2013
Best of Best Award of the Iconic Awards 2013 by the German Design Council, Frankfurt, for the building of the Museum for Architectural Drawing, Berlin
Honourable Mention at the Architectural Review Future Projects Awards 2013, Nice, for the building of the Museum for Architectural Drawing, Berlin

2012
Honourable Mention Award at the XIII Venice Architecture Biennale 2012 for the exhibition *i-city/i-land*
Five Stars, Best Office Architecture at International Property Awards 2012 for the office building at Leninsky prospekt, Moscow
Honourable Mention Award in the Architecture Multiple Residence category at the International Property Awards 2012 for the residential complex Granatny 6, Moscow
Commercial Real Estate St Petersburg Award 2012, Best Business Centre, Class A for the Bank St Petersburg complex, in collaboration with Evgeny Gerasimov and partners, St Petersburg
Architect of the Year, XII Moscow Architecture Biennale and XVII Exhibition for Architecture and Design *Arch Moskva*, in collaboration with Sergey Kuznetsov and SPEECH Tchoban & Kuznetsov, Moscow
Grand Prix and Best Office Award 2012, Best Office for the Director for the interior design of office space for VTB Bank in the west tower of the Federation Complex, Moscow

2011
Immobilien Award Berlin 2011 for Music-und Lifestyle-Hotel nhow, Berlin
International Architecture Award 2011 by the Chicago Athenaeum Museum for Architecture and Design for Hamburger Hof, Berlin
Commendation at the annual exhibition *da!* by the Berlin Chamber of Architects for the modernization and extension of the Hamburger Hof building, Berlin
Ivan-Bazhenov-Medal by the Federation of Architects of Russia
House of the Year 2011, Russia wide readers award for office building at Leninsky prospekt, Moscow
Golden Diploma, First National Glass in Architecture Award for the St Petersburg Plaza complex, in collaboration with Evgeny Gerasimov and partners, St Petersburg
Bronze Diploma, First National Glass in Architecture Award for Langenzipen, St Petersburg

2010
The International Architecture Award 2010 by the Chicago Athenaeum Museum for Architecture and Design for the Cultural Centre and Synagogue Chabad Lubavitch, Berlin

2009
Best House of the Year 2009 of St Petersburg, readers award by Made in Future and Project Baltia magazines for Benois House, St Petersburg
FIABCI Prix d'excellence for Federation Complex, Moscow

2008
Commendation at the annual exhibition *da!* by the Berlin Chamber of Architects for the modernization of Titania Palast building, Berlin
Golden Diploma, Best Realized Project by the Federation of Architects of Russia at the XVI International Zodchestvo 2008 Festival for House at the Sea, St Petersburg, in collaboration with Evgeny Gerasimov and partners, St Petersburg
Commercial Real Estate St Petersburg Award 2008, Best Office Building Class A for Langenzipen, St Petersburg
Silver Diploma of the Federation of Architects of Russia, St Petersburg Section, during the annual Architekton exhibition

2007
Commendation at the annual exhibition *da!* by the Berlin Chamber of Architects for the Cultural Centre and Synagogue Chabad Lubavitch, Berlin and for the modernization of Berolina House, Berlin

2006
Commendation at the annual exhibition *da!* by the Berlin Chamber of Architects for the design of the forecourt at the airport Schönefeld, Berlin, and for the office building Unter den Linden 32-34, Berlin

2005
Honourable Mention at Deutscher Natursteinpreis 2005 for Radisson SAS Hotels DomAquarée, Berlin

2004
Grand Prix by the Federation of Architects of St Petersburg for the draft of the residential complex House by the Sea, St Petersburg, in collaboration with Evgeny Gerasimov and partners, St Petersburg
Commendation at the annual exhibition *da!* by the Berlin Chamber of Architects for Kronprinzenkarree, Berlin
Silver Diploma, Best Planned Building by the Federation of Architects of Russia at the XII International Festival Zodchestvo 2004 for the residential complex House by the Sea, St Petersburg, in collaboration with Evgeny Gerasimov and partners, St Petersburg

2003
Commendation at the annual exhibition *da!* by the Berlin Chamber of Architects for the modernization of the building Kurfürstendamm 42 / Mommsenstraße 71, Berlin, and for the extension of the office space nps tchoban voss Berlin
Experts Award for the co-curation, design and organization of the contribution *Idea, process, space* by Berliner Architektur Union B.A.U. and Aedes Gallery Berlin for the VIII Arch Moskva Exhibition of Architecture and Environmental Design, in collaboration with Kuehn Bauer Partner, AssmannSalomon, Kiefer, Leonhardt, Andrä and Partner and Meuser Architekten BDA

2002
Commendation at the German Interior Design Award by the Federation of German Interior Designers BDIA for Cubix, Berlin, in collaboration with Schwitzke and Partner, Düsseldorf
Commendation at the annual exhibition *da!* by the Berlin Chamber of Architects for Cubix, Berlin

2000
Experts Award for curating, design and organization of the contribution *Space for Art* at the V Arch Moskva Exhibition of Architecture and Environmental Design
Multiple Awards of Excellence, Architecture in Perspective by American Society of Architectural Illustrators for architectural drawings (1992–1999, 2001, 2004, 2006–2008, 2010, 2012, 2013, 2014).

Exhibitions

2014
This is modern, participation, Deutsche Werkbund exhibition during the XIV Venice Architecture Biennale 2014, Venice
All about Italy!, participation, Stately Tretyakov-Gallery, Moscow

2013
Northern Vision, participation, Sir John Soane's Museum, London
Architectural drawing, exhibition for Architecture and Design *Arch Moskva* 2013, Moscow

2012
12 Architects Design Furniture, participation in the Orgatec 2012 fair trade with office collection for furniture manufacturer Nayada, Cologne
Moscow Design Week, participation with the art installation *Architect's Eye*, Moscow
i-city/i-land, curation, design, organization and participation in the exhibition of the Russian Pavilion at the XIII Venice Architecture Biennale 2012, Venice; catalogue published
Interni Legacy, participation with the art installation *Architect's Eye* during the Milan Design Week, Milan
MIPIM 2012, participation in the Moscow stand, Cannes
Moscow Design Week, participation with the installation *Architect's eye*

2011
Evgeny Gerasimov and partners XX, participation, St Petersburg
XIX International Zodchestvo Festival 2011, participation, Moscow
Reliquari, Musivum Gallery, participation during the Artplay fair trade, Moscow
Architektura Peterburga 2011, participation during the III Biennale for Contemporary Architecture, The Russian Museum of Ethnography, St Petersburg
MIPIM 2011, participation in the Moscow stand, Cannes
Duravit Design Days 2011, participation with the Esplanade series of sanitary accessories, Duravit Design Center, Hornberg

2010
Factory Russia, co-curation, design, organization and participation in the exhibition of the Russian Pavilion at the XII Venice Architecture Biennale, Venice; catalogue published
The Golden Age of Architectural Graphics, participation, Pushkin Museum of Fine Arts, Moscow; catalogue published
II Moscow Architecture Biennale 2010, participation, Moscow
Architectural Worlds. Sergei Tchoban Draftsman and Collector, solo exhibition, Deutsches Architekturmuseum DAM, Frankfurt

2009
Emergency Reserve. Industrial Architecture of the Past – a Resource for the Future, curation and participation as part of the XVII International Zodchestvo Festival 2009, Manege exhibition hall, Moscow
European Embankment, design, organization and participation with the Europe Embankment project, St Petersburg, Galerie Aedes Pfefferberg, Berlin; catalogue published
Die Wiederentdeckung Sretenkas (The Rediscovery Sretenka), design, organization and participation, Galerie AedesLand, Berlin; catalogue published
nps tchoban voss – Internationale Projekte, design and organization in line with the Hamburger Architektursommer 2009 festival, Fachbuchhandlung Sautter + Lackmann, Hamburg
RodDom ("Birth of the House"), participation, Lille
Aqua, solo exhibition, Galleria Antonia Jannone, Milan; catalogue published
Modernisierung der Platte. Erfahrungen aus Deutschland ("Modernizing the Slab. Experiences from Germany"), participation, St Petersburg; catalogue published
Gorod i dom ("City and House"), participation, St Petersburg

2008
Aura designa, participation, St Petersburg
Sergei Tchoban – Petersburger Hängung ("Salon Hang") solo exhibition, Galerie Werkraum Berlin
Berlin Moscow, solo exhibition, Sochi Art Museum, Sochi
sergei tchoban - zeichnen planen bauen ("drawing planning building"), solo exhibition, Deutsche Werkstätten Hellerau, Dresden
Architekturachse Russland-Deutschland ("Architectural Axis Russia-Germany"), solo exhibition during the German Week festival, together with Evgeny Gerasimov and partners St Petersburg, Building of the Federation of Architects, St Petersburg

2007
RodDom ("Birth of the House"), participation, St Petersburg; catalogue published
Architektur für die Stadt, Peter Schweger und Sergei Tchoban ("Architecture for the City"), solo exhibition together with Prof Peter Schweger, The Russian Academy of Arts, St Petersburg
XII Arch Moskva Exhibition for Architecture and Design, participation, Central House of the Artist, Moscow

2006
Federation Tower. Prof Peter Schweger and Sergei Tchoban, solo exhibition together with Prof Peter Schweger, Deutsches Architekturzentrum DAZ, Berlin
High Society. Aktuelle Hochhausarchitektur und der Internationale Hochhaus Preis 2006 ("Today's High-Rise Architecture and the International High-Rise Award"), participation in collaboration with Prof Peter Schweger, Deutsches Architekturmuseum DAM, Frankfurt; catalogue published

2005
Berlin–Moskau – Москва–Берлин, solo exhibition, Galerie Aedes-East, Berlin; catalogue published
Playground, participation, ArtPlay Architecture- and Design Centre, Moscow
Peter Schweger. Sergei Tchoban. Federation Tower, solo exhibition in collaboration with Prof Peter Schweger, Shchusev State Museum of Architecture, Moscow

2004
Berlin im Fluss ("Berlin Flowing"), participation, Shchusev State Museum of Architecture, Moscow
Moskauer Archäologie ("Moscow Archaeology"), solo exhibition, Shchusev State Museum of Architecture, Moscow
Moscow-Berlin. Architecture 1950–2000, curation and participation, Shchusev State Museum of Architecture, Moscow
STADTanSICHTEN – Planschrank Moskau ("City Sights – Moscow Plan Chest"), curation, design, organization and participation, ifa-Galerie Berlin, Bonn, Stuttgart; catalogue published

2003
Idee, Prozess, Raum ("Idea, Process, Space") contribution to the VIII Arch Moskva Exhibition for Architecture and Environmental Design for Berliner Architektur Union B.A.U. and Galerie Aedes Berlin, with Kuehn Bauer Partner, AssmannSalomon, Kiefer, Leonhardt, Andrä und Partner and Meuser Architekten, co-curation, design, organization and participation, Moscow
50 Projects of new Berlin, co-curation, design and organization, Shchusev State Museum of Architecture, Moscow
Interarch 2003, participation in the anniversary exhibition of the academic council of the International Academy of Architecture Moscow MAAM presenting best Moscow architects out of competition during the International Triennale, Sofia

2002
Alexander Brodski: An Installation, curation and organization, Galerie Aedes East Extension Pavilion, Berlin
Valery Koshlyakov: PackageBandGlassPalace, curation and organization, Galerie Aedes East Extension Pavilion, Berlin

2000
Raum für Kunst ("Space for Art"), curation, design and organization des contribution to the V Arch Moskva Exhibition for Architecture and Environmental Design, Moscow

1999
Five Drawn Worlds – Fünf gezeichnete Welten, curation, design, organization and participation, Galerie Aedes East, Berlin; catalogue published

1997
Sergei Tchoban and the Java-Tower, solo exhibition, Galerie Aedes East, Berlin; catalogue published

1995
Drawing the Future ("Gezeichnete Architektur"), solo exhibition together with Frank Constantino, Galerie Aedes West, Berlin
A Perspectivist Salon, participation, School of Interior Design, New York

1993
XIII International Exhibition of the American Society of Architectural Illustrators, participation, Tokyo, Nagoya

1990
Architekturdarstellung und Architekturvisionen ("Architectural Illustration and Architectural Visions") participation upon invitation of BDA Hamburg, Fachhochschule Hamburg

1988–1991
Architecture and applied arts, participation, Moscow; catalogue published
Young Artists of St Petersburg, design of the exhibition on 1,500 sq m, St Petersburg
Young Artists of St Petersburg, design of the exhibition on 4,500 sq m, Central House of the Artist, Moscow

1986–1988
Participation with architectural drawings in several exhibitions in St Petersburg, Moscow and Prague
da!, annual exhibition by the Berlin Chamber of Architects (participations in 2014, 2012, 2008, 2007, 2006, 2004, 2003, 2002; catalogues published)
Architecture in Perspective, annual exhibition of the American Society of Architectural Illustrators, participation with architectural drawings in exhibitions (29/2014, 28/2013, 27/2012, 25/2010, 23/2008, 22/2007, 21/2006, 16/2001, 15/2000, 14/1999, 13/1998, 10/1995, 9/1994, 8/1993, 7/1992 in several cities in the US and Canada; catalogues published)